£2

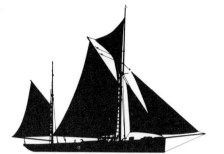

Tops´l Books

9, Queen Victoria Street, Reading, England.

STEAM FISHERMEN
in old photographs

The story of the glorious age of steam drifters and trawlers and the men who sailed them, told with over 50 old photographs from the unique Ford Jenkins collection.

Cover Picture

● The last surviving steam drifter *YH89 Lydia Eva* on her last voyage. Lydia Eva was built in steel at Kings Lynn in 1930 for Harry Eastick of Great Yarmouth. She is 104ft long, 20ft beam and 143 net tonnage with a triple expansion boiler relying on natural draught only. Her fishing career lasted until the outbreak of war in 1939 when she was bought by the R.A.F. for towing targets and similar duties. When she was due for the breakers yard in 1969 the Maritime Trust bought her for restoration with the help of a gift of £4,000 from Sir Cyril Kleinwort, in memory of the steam drifter men with whom he served at Scapa Flow during the war. Attempts to keep her open to the public in her home port proved uneconomical and the Trust reluctantly moved her to a final berth at St. Katharine's Dock, London where she can now be seen. The photograph was taken on her last voyage from Great Yarmouth.

Title Page

● *LT681 Sincere* bucks her way seawards out of Lowestoft. A wooden drifter, 86ft overall, 43 net tons and 30 h.p. built for Chalkie Westgate in 1916. Her oval truck marks her as having come from the Richards yard in Lowestoft. She was later owned by Seven Limited.

Opposite

● Drifters leaving Lowestoft just after the First World War. Astern of the line is *LT1262 Lisburn,* 48 tons net, built at Oulton Broad in 1917 for the Herring Fishery Company Limited.

The Fishing Photographers

FOR OVER 80 YEARS the Jenkins family of Lowestoft have been photographing the East Coast fishing fleets whose comings and goings can be seen from their studio. The combined work of three generations of them makes a unique and valuable record of the fortunes of the British fishing industry and the communities whose livelihood depended on it.

The collection began in 1896 when Harry Jenkins, already the son of a photographer, arrived in Lowestoft to set up business for himself. Lofty masts and brown tanned sails predominated and steam was only just becoming a serious challenge. His son, Ford Jenkins, carried on the business and his camera was busy through the great heyday of steam chronicled in this book. Today the grandson, Peter Jenkins, photographs a much contracted modern trawler fleet (the herring drifter having entirely gone from the East Coast) and more of his work is now in connection with oil rigs and their support vessels.

The first volume in this series "Sailing Fishermen In Old Photographs", was based mainly on the work of Harry Jenkins, with that of Ford Jenkins illustrating the declining days of sail. Happily in this second title the work of all three generations comes together. Grandfather Jenkins recorded on glass plate the growth of steam up to the beginning of the First World War, and Ford Jenkins followed its fortunes through the 20's and 30's and its declining days after that. The cover picture which marks the final farewell of steam fishing is by Peter Jenkins.

This introduction would not be complete without mention of another member of the Jenkins family, Cdr. Ralph Jenkins, O.B.E., D.S.C. R.N. Rtd., who, as President of the Lowestoft & East Suffolk Maritime Society, has been a driving force in the development of the Lowestoft Maritime Museum as a lasting reminder to the splendid race of fishermen who lived in both the age of sail and steam. He and many of his fellow members have given valuable help with information for this book, as, of course, have Mr. Ford and Mr. Peter Jenkins.

For anyone interested in following this subject further the Museum at Sparrow's Nest, Lowestoft and the Jenkins studio at 11, The Bridge, Lowestoft are well worth a visit.

The Change from Sail to Steam

IN THE GOLDEN October sunshine of 1913 the quaysides of the East Anglian ports were piled shoulder high with fish. Steam drifters in their hundreds packed the harbours of Lowestoft and Great Yarmouth in one solid mass, the local boats almost outnumbered by the Scottish fleets from Buckie, Banff, Kircaldy and a dozen other tiny ports.

Looking across the rows of tall thin funnels one thing was evident to every fisherman's eye. This bumper harvest was the harvest of steam. The tall masts and tanned sails of the dandy rigged drifters on which 19th century herring fortunes had been built now made up less than a fifth of the vessels jostling and manoeuvring for a berth alongside the fish quays.

As if to mark the irrecoverable ascendancy of steam over sail, this great fleet of coal burners was landing the hugest catch of herring ever known. The fishing ports of Britain, particularly along the North Sea coast, were used to record breaking landings, for the fishing industry had been growing lustily for half a century, ever since steam on land, in the shape of the railways, had opened up a market among the mushrooming populations of industrial Britain. The harvest of 1913 beat them all. Over half a million tons of herring were caught in that year. But they accounted for only half the total amount of fish. The trawler fleets, also now dominated by steam vessels, landed massive catches of cod, plaice and other demersal or bottom feeding fish from the still prolific grounds of the North Sea and beyond.

So great was the accumulation of fish at Lowestoft and Yarmouth that the market and the curers could not cope and skippers were ordered away by their owners to try selling their catches further up the coast at Grimsby or Scarborough.

1913 was a memorable year for the steam fishermen, but it was also the turning point. Nobody was ever again to see such a vast harvest of fish, or such a crowded harbour. Both steam vessels and the British fishing industry had reached their zenith. In less than a year the fishermen celebrating in the dockside pubs had traded their red ensigns for white ensigns and were fishing for mines. When they returned it was to a dwindling world. They never made such hauls again, nor could they have guessed how quickly their sturdy steam trawlers and drifters, in 1913 the epitome of modern technology, would follow mast and sail into obsolescence.

While the British Isles were covered with a network of steam railways during Queen Victoria's reign the new motive power was much slower reaching the fishing fleets. Practicable steam engines had been around since 1705 when Newcomen perfected the first for pumping out Cornish tin mines, but it was a hundred years before one reliably powered a ship, and another three quarters of a century after that before they were successfuly used for fishing.

● Silhouetted between the Lowestoft pierheads in the last of the evening light. A common East Coast scene in the first quarter of this century.

The problem of early marine steam engines was one of payload. They were so huge and needed so much coal and water that the first steamships were fully laden with their own fuel and engine before they set off, and could scarcely raise enough speed to stem the tide let alone carry a cargo. Improvements followed Watt's invention, in 1769, of the condenser which increased the amount of work done by the piston and turned steam into efficient motive power. Ironically, although his inventive genius was responsible more than any other single step for driving the horse from the road and the sail from the sea, Watt himself opposed the idea of steam being used for anything other than a stationary engine.

He was not without fellow sceptics. As late as 1830, 17 years after Bell's *Comet* (locally known as The Stink Pot) had successfully steamed down the Clyde with a piper on the foredeck, and 16 years after the *Margery* had steamed across the Channel, Rear-Admiral Baron de Raigersfield, R.N. gave his assessment of steamships: "It appears all humbug", he wrote, "for one broadside would annihilate such presumption".

It was a view shared by other naval officers for a long time to come. A common opinion was that steamers were alright for harbour and estuary work but unfit for sea. This was partly because most of the early steamships were driven by paddle wheels which are excellent in confined waters, as they can be turned in a very tight circle by disengaging the shaft of one wheel. Also, unlike a screw vessel, they have as much power going astern as going forward. A rolling open sea on the other hand places great strain on the engines of a paddler. Though the British Admiralty may be accused of being slow to adopt a new idea it was certainly faithful to it once committed, for Their Lordships built two paddlers as tugs, for which work they were excellent, after the Second World War, not many years before they built their first nuclear submarine.

The first steam fishing vessels were also paddlers. They were in fact converted tugs. The story of how that came about is precisely chronicled.

Since around the 1860's steam paddle tugs had been employed to give sailing smacks and luggers a pluck out of harbour when contrary or light winds made it impossible for them to sail out. In some instances when there was a flat calm, tugs would tow smacks to some of the nearer fishing grounds. This is what the tug *Messenger* did for a smack out of North Shields, then a considerable fishing port, in November 1877.

Now a sailing smack needed a good breeze in her sails to tow a trawl along the seabed, so in a calm she could not work and on this occasion the smack's skipper asked the tug to continue the tow while he shot his trawl and fished. After a time the tug captain, William Purdy, began to wonder at the logic of towing a smack which was towing a trawl. Might he not as well be towing the trawl himself? As times were lean for tug work on Tyneside William Purdy thought there would be no harm in trying the experiment. That winter he bought some secondhand trawl nets and gear and fitted out his ageing paddler as a trawler. The local smacksmen derided his efforts and told him he would lose his money with such an impossible idea. They reminded him that previous attempts to fish with steam vessels, made in one or two places in the 1860's had failed. When Purdy's paddles thrashed out of the Tyne on his first trip it was to the sound of jeers and catcalls.

Nevertheless the *Messenger's* maiden venture made a modest profit and her second one an even better. There was a rush to fit out unemployed paddle tugs with beam trawls. Within a year or so 50 paddle tugmasters had followed Purdy's example and the idea spread rapidly down the east coast to Scarborough, Grimsby and beyond. Steam had proved it could catch fish and after that it rapidly changed the face of the fishing industry. It also sowed the seeds of its demise. That was something the fish merchants of North Shields could not foresee when they presented William Purdy with a gold watch for his enterprise.

● Running before an easterly gale into Lowestoft's 130ft wide entrance was one operation at least slightly less treacherous for the steam drifters than for their sailing predecessors. Here the wooden drifter *LT396 United* negotiates the confused seas between the piers. The funnel in front of the wheelhouse indicates she is a fairly early steamer and was in fact built at Lowestoft in 1901, owned by Noah Ayres. The first steam drifters had tiller steering with no shelter for the helmsman. When the change to wheel steering was made the wheelhouses were placed abaft the funnel because there were problems with making a long linkage between the rudder head and the steering gear, though this obviously did not improve the helmsman's visibility. Judging by the amount of bag o'wrinkle on the forestay *United* obviously still made good use of her foresail. These were abandoned later, but the spar remained for use as a derrick when unloading. The mizzen sail remained to keep the vessel steady in the wind when fishing.

Once the success of these improvised steam trawlers was known it was naturally not long before steamships were built for the purpose and then thoughts turned to the propeller as a more efficient means of propulsion than the paddle wheel. Paddlers were at home on the inshore grounds, but the turbulent seas of the Dogger and other more distant North Sea grounds were no place for them. The fishing career of steam paddle-ships was quickly over as the yards pressed on apace with orders for screw steam fishing vessels. Only one port remained faithful to the paddlers and that was Scarborough where they survived until about 1904.

The first of this new breed was probably the *Zodiac* laid down in Erle's yard in Hull in 1881 for a new company set up to stake a claim in the new technology — the Grimsby & North Sea Steam Trawling Company. Barring her funnel the *Zodiac* looked like any other big first class smack, ketch rigged and carrying a full suit of sails, but below was a compound surface condensing engine developing 35 h.p. A sister ship the *Aries* quickly followed her down the ways and the two were so profitable that the company ordered four more the following year. In fact it must be a tribute to the original designer that the same firm eventually bought 160 other trawlers of the same class.

These modern wonders were costing their owners just over £3,500 a piece, well over twice the cost of a first class smack which could be had at the time ready for sea at £1,500. Nevertheless, bigger trawler owners were eager to be in the fashion and newly launched sailing smacks were sold off cheap to make way for steam replacements. Iron hulls ousted the traditional wooden carvel build and costs soared. Ten years after the launch of the *Zodiac* 2,000 steam trawlers had been built in Britain and by that time they were costing £10,000.

Hull was a little slower off the mark than its rival across the Humber, but more than made up for lost time. The first steam trawler appeared in the Yorkshire port in 1884 and by 1900 every one of the 450 sailing smacks had been ousted. The story was similar in Grimsby where two or three dozen smacks survived among the sprouting funnels just a few years longer.

Similar developments were going on in Scotland. The first Scottish steam fishing vessel is believed to have been the long liner of Leith, *LH92 Rob Roy* launched in 1882. She was 56ft long, built on the lines of a fifie, but with a cut down suit of sails and an inverted two stage expansion type engine which gave her a speed of eight knots.

The same year saw the first Scottish purpose built steam trawler, also built in Leith. She was the *Hawk*, 87ft long with a two stage expansion engine with 13" and 14" cylinders with an 18" stroke. Like all the early steam trawlers she was a belt and braces job rigged for sailing too, just in case this new fangled machinery should prove unreliable, and in this respect the *Hawk* was a bit of an oddity for she was schooner rigged, a rig very uncommon indeed for a British fishing vessel.

The fact that these rapid changes took place in Northern ports was an accident of geology. The price of coal was in direct proportion to its distance from the pithead. Along the coastline adjacent to the coalfields of Yorkshire, Durham and Lanarkshire it was to be had in cheap abundance, as cheap and abundant as the fish it helped to catch. Men toiled and risked their lives for both without hope of benefiting overmuch from this economic miracle that steam fishing was about to bring. But the directors of the railway companies must have been on their knees in heartfelt thanksgiving. Having invested heavily in lines and dock installations to attract the fish traffic between the ports and the inland industrial towns, they now had a guaranteed freight in both directions. They carried the cod that fed the miners that dug the coal that powered the ships that caught the cod that . . . .

It was the use of steam paddle tugs to give sailing smacks a pluck out of harbour in calm or contrary winds which led directly to the first adoption of steam power for fishing. The Great Eastern Railway's harbour tug is towing *LT263 Paradigm*, *LT382 Gertrude* and *LT445 Myrtle* all of which are in various stages of hoisting their foresails ready to cast off the tow and bear away up the deep water channel. Over the smack's port quarters can be seen the beam trawls which the sailing fishermen continued to use, though the steam trawlermen universally adopted the more capacious otter trawl. All three smacks were built around 1890.

So it was that Yarmouth, Lowestoft, Ramsgate and Brixham waited quite a few years longer for the benefits of steam. Neither was the headlong rush of the trawler owners of Scotland and Northern England shared by other countries. In 1909 it was reported that the ports of Hull and Grimsby each had more steam trawlers on the register than all the other countries bordering the North Sea put together. At that time Germany was the nearest rival for fishing power with 290 steam trawlers, Holland had 78, Belgium 25, Norway 15, Denmark 15 and France 10, a total of 433 compared with the 1,336 then registered in England and Wales.

So far the story has been about developments in trawling. Steam was slower coming to the drifters and less well documented. In anything to do with the fishing industry the two sections must always be considered separately for they are quite distinct, each with its own problems and tending to be two distinct communities even when sharing the same port.

It was not until 1897, Queen Victoria's Diamond Jubilee Year, that the first steam drifter was built at Lowestoft, *LT718 Consolation*, by the Chambers & Colby yard, for Mr. George Catchpole of Kessingland. She had tiller steering and a full suit of sails on a wooden hull and, except for a small funnel placed well aft, looked just like any other herring lugger.

There had certainly been earlier steam drifters bought by Yarmouth and Lowestoft owners from Scottish and Tyneside yards but it was not until after the launch of the *Consolation* that steam began to make its mark in the herring fleets. A Scottish writer said that the herring fishermen were intensely proud of the smart appearance of their boats and could not tolerate them being covered in filthy coal dust, but economic factors were more probably the influencing factor. For one thing there was not the same financial incentive since a drifter was not quite so reliant on the vagaries of the wind as a trawler smack, being able to lie to her nets and be catching in a calm which put a stop to trawling. Neither did the drifter, working much nearer port, have such distances to cover against contrary winds. Also drifters tended more to be owned by individual skippers, or small family syndicates unable to find capital to go into steam in those early days when a cautious bank manager might have thought it a gamble. Soon, however, the bank managers were doing some simple arithmetic based on the equation that a ton of coal at Lowestoft cost £1 which was equal to the average price fetched by one cran of herring, a cran being equal to about 3½ cwts.

● In the heyday of steam fishing harbour entrances like Lowestoft were busy crossroads. Three Scottish drifters down for the autumn season are leaving harbour, in company with two sailing trawler smacks in the far distance and one sailing drifter to the right. Overhauling the smacks is one of the regular steam freighters which took herring to the Continent, while coming in on the left is the steam barge *Pioneer* which was constantly at work dumping sand from the dredger which kept the port from silting up. In the foreground is *BF1140 The Colonel*, a 34 ton wooden drifter of 40 h.p. built at Banff in 1908 for J.J. George & Partners of Macduff. Below, the drifter *LT125 Homeland* on her trials in 1908. When war broke out in 1914 she was fishing off the Shetlands and on returning home was requisitioned for minesweeping.

The early powered drifters cost something over £2,000 a time, fully equipped, compared with not much over £450 previously paid for a sailing drifter, but once the *Consolation* had led the way, despite a troublesome boiler, money was soon forthcoming. Luggers were laid up or scrapped by the hundred. Within two or three years of launching the *Consolation* Chambers had taken their last order for a sailing drifter. By 1903 Lowestoft had 100 steam drifters registered and their success at catching fish and landing it fast for a profitable market was such that the 622 luggers belonging to the port in 1906 had been reduced to 152 by 1914. Most of those were broken up for war scrap and not one survived to fish again after the war ended in 1918.

Though entering the steam age generally 15 years behind their trawler brethren, the English herring fishermen had made a clean sweep of things in 17 years. In Scotland by 1910 they had built a thousand ships to replace almost half the sailing fleet. Of the sturdy black sailed zulus and fifies with their ancient dipping lugsails (for the Scottish fishermen never accepted the gaff rig common in England after 1860) about 100 worked into the 1920's and a solitary couple until the mid 1930's.

The conversion of the trawler fleets, though started earlier, was in the end not so total. A few sailing trawler smacks continued fishing until the outbreak of the Second World War in 1939 and new ones were being built as late as the 1920's. For this there was a reason. Drifters, whether sail or steam, caught herring and mackerel which was no different in quality. The effect of steam trawling on the other hand was to produce bigger catches at the expense of quality and consequently there remained a demand for sail caught white fish, fetching a higher price, which a few skippers were content to satisfy.

When the *Consolation* was launched many Lowestoft folk were surprised that it was not the rival yard across the way owned by the flamboyant Sam Richards which had won the race into the new age. Twenty years before he had worked his passage from Cornwall with 25 gold sovereigns in his pocket and started a ship building business which continues today. But Sam was biding his time. He had seen that steam would be no passing fancy and was preparing to launch into it properly by building his own engine construction sheds instead of installing machinery bought elsewhere. While he was about it he fitted the engine sheds with the first electric light in East Anglia.

In 1899 he was ready and launched the *Adventure,* bought by a Mr. Trip, and the *Test* for Messrs. C. & R. Harvey of Kessingland. Both were 78ft long with tiller steering and a full suit of sails. After that Richards' never built another purely sailing drifter, although they continued to build smacks until 1924.

In the race into steam drifters that followed this one yard alone built 100 of them before the outbreak of the First World War. For the shipwrights, working 12 hours a day every day except Sunday, the pace must have been a hot one. The most notable achievement was the completion of the *Briton* in 1906 in 40 working days from keel laying to maiden voyage. She could steam at 10½ knots and was obviously none the worse for the haste in building, as she subsequently made the trip from Lowestoft to Penzance for the West Country mackerel season in 44 hours.

Sam Richards celebrated this new wave of prosperity by becoming the first man in Lowestoft to own one of the new fangled motor cars.

● The first steam driven drifter built at Lowestoft *LT718 Consolation* ready for launching. At the tiller is probably her owner Mr. George "Mouse" Catchpole of Kessingland. Though the first steam drifter to be launched in the Suffolk port, she was almost certainly not the first to fish from it. A few bought from Scotland and Tyneside were working out of Yarmouth and Lowestoft some years before the *Consolation*.

The Life of the Steam Fishermen

THE GENERAL conversion from sail to steam involved far more than a change of motive power. It effected almost everything about the industry — methods, manning, profits, wages — and not always for the better. One thing the steam revolution effected surprisingly little was the hazards and hardships of the job. Fishing continued to be one of the toughest and most dangerous means of breadwinning on earth.

One of the first changes evident to the fishing crews was a new shipmate. Men skilled with sheet and halliard were no match for the mechanical monster they now bore in the bowels of their boat. They needed an engineer, or 'driver' as he was quickly christened, assisted by a fireman or 'trimmer'. Large trawlers also carried a second engineer.

Any thought that the engine room staff had an easier time of it than the men hauling and shooting nets in all weathers on deck can be dismissed. Walter Wood, a well known writer on the fishing industry just before and after the First World War, describes how, "in hot or bad weather they had a persistently uncomfortable time. Heavy rolls and pitches made the very body ache in attempts to keep a footing and to escape being hurled into the moving machinery or against the red hot furnace. Battened down in a steam trawler, notorious for sea shipping (often known as a 'washer'), there was the added misery of poisonous air to breathe".

For enduring these conditions in 1910 the chief engineer of a trawler was earning an average of 46 shillings (£2.30) a week, his second 36 shillings (£1.80) a week and the trimmer, rated at the bottom of the scale with the cook and deckies, averaged 24 shillings (£1.20) a week. There was a shortage of competent engineers, to the great concern of owners who had a valuable capital tied up in the machinery of their vessels and were anxious for its proper care. There was little inducement for engineers in the merchant service with Board of Trade certificates to join the fishing fleets. On the other hand the qualifications required for the certificate made it difficult for engine room staff in trawlers and drifters without other experience to gain one. If the situation worried the owners it worried their insurers even more. Consequently, in 1910 the insurance companies set up their own system of examinations. Since the scheme was operated from Aberdeen, the insurers of which City had taken the initiative, the award became known as the Aberdeen Certificate and for more than a decade afterwards holders of it were much sought after by steam trawler and drifter companies.

It was not surprising that the Board of Trade did not consider it necessary to certify fishing vessel engineers, for it had only a few years before made it compulsory for skippers to have a 'ticket'. Steam was responsible for this change too. When the majority of sailing smacks were on the North Sea banks, not 50 or 60 miles from home, examinations for skippers were considered unnecessary, as well as difficult to arrange as many of these fine seamen could not read or write. It became a different story when steam trawlers were working 1,000 miles away on the Arctic Circle in the depths of winter. Then the strain on trawler skippers became immense. For that matter it still is.

● *Consolation* under construction in Chambers yard. Framing has been completed and planking just commenced. Her build was exactly that of a sailing drifter with a space left in the hold for the engine and vertical boiler and a cement lined bulkhead which protected the rest of the ship from the heat. The launching into Lake Lothing at Lowestoft involved an ingenious system of round and hollow blocks along which the vessel was hauled to the waters edge with a horse driven windlass.

Apart from the responsibility for navigation on long voyages and the need to be a commercially successful fish finder, skippers took only the briefest snatches of sleep for days on end when on the grounds. Often they were, like footballers, finished at 35. By that time the lucky ones with a succession of good seasons might have made a comfortable nest egg entirely by share of net profits. But by no means all were so fortunate. A report of 1910 put a trawler skipper's average weekly earnings at £4, though this was twice as much as the mate's who only averaged 35 to 40 shillings a week, and three times as much as third hands at 27 shillings (£1.35). In a particularly bad year one Lowestoft trawler skipper earned £34 for the whole year's work. About the same time Yarmouth's most successful herring skipper made £200 in the year, the earnings of the boat having been £3,400.

Such were the vagaries of the share system that the crew's remuneration was not always truly reflected in what the vessel earned. Shares were paid on net earnings after the running costs of the voyage, including capital allowances, had been deducted. Some companies were adept at stringing out these expenses. Some were also reluctant to let anyone see the detailed figures, though skippers and mates had a legal entitlement to see them as their earnings depended entirely on share without any element of fixed wage. A Parliamentary Committee in 1932 heard evidence of men being victimised for questioning the settlement, and even of the fish market auctions being rigged to the disadvantage of the men. It was even known for running expense deductions to exceed catch earnings and a man could finish up after hard weeks of fishing with nothing — or worse, actually in debt to his employers. It has to be said for the owners that such debts were seldom claimed.

Up to 1925 there was another nasty twist to the share system. Those who were remunerated in this way were legally regarded as self employed and could not qualify for unemployment pay, sickness benefit, or compensation for industrial injury. But the change from sail to steam had not altered the traditional independence of fishermen. They generally resisted suggestions of abolishing the share system in favour of a fixed wage. There remained the alluring gamble of one day fetching port with a bumper catch and hitting the jackpot while auction prices were still high.

It would be wrong to say that the change to steam brought no improvement in working conditions, but they were few and slow to come. The first was the replacement of the tiller with a wheel, followed by a wheelhouse to give the helmsman shelter. Later there came the addition of a galley, a luxury previously unknown at least on the drifters where meals were cooked and eaten on the knee in a tiny box-like common cabin.

Working on deck men were at least relieved of hoisting and trimming sails, but off duty below many thought themselves worse off in steam. Though the motion of a sailing vessel in a heavy sea can be violent, it is more comfortable than the headlong pitching of a steamer which makes it difficult to sleep in a bunk, especially one located over the constant juddering of the propeller shaft.

A change for the worse for many trawlermen was the increase in "fleeting" which was a consequential result of the shift to steam. The pernicious practice of fleeting had been carried out in the bigger ports with sailing smacks for many years, ever since the boom in fishing in the later decades of the 19th century had attracted outside capital into the industry.

Smacks owned by their skippers or small local syndicates in places like Lowestoft always went "single boating", that is to say fishing on their own. In ports like Hull and Grimsby where limited liability companies acquired big fleets of smacks it was found more profitable to send them to sea together under the command of an experienced skipper or "admiral" with a reputation for smelling where the fish were. He ordered each smack by signal (flags by day and rockets by night) where and when to shoot and when to haul, even on what tack they should trawl.

● Sea trials following launching and fitting out, when wives and families went for the trip, made memorable social occasions for the fishermen. Bureaucracy later put a stop to these on the grounds of safety, though there seems to be no record of any mishap occurring. This was in 1908 at the commissioning of *LT109 Bon Espoir* a wooden Lowestoft built drifter of 39 net tons. Mr. E. Pye of Lowestoft who qualified as a 'driver' or engineer around 1919 remembers she had what was nicknamed a 'monkey engine'. It was a triple expansion engine built by Elliott and Garrood and got its name because the high pressure chamber sat on top of the intermediate chamber in a way vaguely reminiscent of an organ grinder's monkey. Despite its name it made the *Bon Espoir* a very fast boat. Elliott engines, made locally at Beccles, were reckoned among the best.

Each fleet, consisting of approximately 50 smacks spread out in a great seven mile circle, had its own steam carrier waiting to fill up with the day's catch and rush it to market. In this way there was no need for the trawlers to make wasteful journeys to and from port. They could stay longer on the grounds where their catching capacity could be fully employed. As an exercise in cost effectiveness it was perfect. As a way of life it was hell. Instead of a seven or ten day trip men faced four weeks of constant grind. The only comforts off watch were the cramped confines of a stuffy cabin and the indifferent efforts of an amateur cook dishing out suet dumplings and over boiled mutton. Worst of all was the hazardous business of transferring the catch to the carriers. Each trawler's crew had to ferry its own fish in large trunks loaded in their own small dinghy and often with a terrible sea running. This operation cost many lives.

Logically it might be supposed that fleeting would have ended with the coming of steam, when trawlers could now make a straight course and steady speed to market regardless of the wind. This did not prove the case. Fleet owners found that their steam ships could be better organised in the system than the smacks and productivity improved even further. So fleeting increased and with it the dangers of the job.

Though steamers should have been safer in many respects than smacks, the annual statistics remained monotonously similar through sail and steam for 20 or 30 years after they were first recorded in 1884. Before that it had not been legally necessary even to report deaths and drownings at sea. The returns for 1910 showed that there were 107,719 fishermen at sea and 241 had been lost in the year, a rate of one in every 427. But that was taking the industry as a whole. The death rate on trawlers was more than twice as bad. One trawlerman in every 203 was killed by accident or drowning. Nothing among the shore industries, not even mining, could compete for mortality.

Some of the changes that followed steam brought new dangers with them. Steel wire trawl warps replaced hemp rope. In bad sea conditions these could tauten suddenly and sever a limb or afflict a fatal gash. More powerful double barrel steel winches which replaced capstans also claimed victims who were caught up in them. Acetylene replaced oil lamps and the drums of chemical which fuelled these sometimes exploded. As trawlers searched ever more northerly latitudes it was found that ice could form so thick and so fast on the top hamper that its weight could roll a ship over before men could hack it away with axes.

● Above, *LT140 Alcore* trawling. The trawl warps can be seen leading away from the gallows on the port side, while the starboard set of otter boards not in use are hoisted up. The basket at the forestay warns other vessels she has her gear down and should be given a wide berth. On deck, aft, both stoker and cook have come up for a breather. Below, Trials of the steam drifter *LT750 Supernal* in 1910 with this time only one finely dressed lady aboard. The man on top of the wheelhouse is the compass adjuster taking bearings from which his colleague at the binnacle below can correct deviation.

One totally unexpected and fortunately isolated danger came to the Gamecock fleet of steam trawlers, so named for the company's bird emblem on the funnels.

Fishing the Dogger on a clear October night in 1904 they found themselves suddenly, without warning, under shell and machine gun fire from four Russian battleships. Startled skippers rang for full steam and ordered the trawl warps to be cut in a vain effort to escape a concerted ten minute bombardment. Then the Imperial Navy slipped away into the night as quickly and mysteriously as it had come. In the Gamecock fleet one trawler, the *Crane*, was going down, her skipper and third hand dead. Several more trawlers were badly damaged and six other men injured, one fatally.

It was ten days before anyone on Humberside knew why the Tzar's ships had shelled the innocent fishing vessels of a friendly power in international waters. Russia at the time was at war with Japan. The Admiral of the Baltic Squadron, finding himself in the night in the midst of a large number of small vessels had rashly assumed he was surrounded by Japanese torpedo boats and, without waiting to confirm his suspicions, immediately gave the order to open fire. After two years of diplomatic wrangling some compensation was eventually paid by the Russian government amounting to £60,000 for loss and damage. The widows received about £2,000 each, which was a fortune compared with the miserable few pounds they would have had from local friendly societies and charitable whip-rounds if their husbands had been simply drowned at sea.

Undoubtedly the greatest change that came in the wake of steam was the introduction of the otter trawl. The expansion of the sailing smacks from the middle of the 19th century had been based on the development of the beam trawl, the beam being a 30 to 40 foot long spar of beech, oak or elm which kept open the mouth of the great triangular bag of the trawl as it was dragged along the bottom. In place of the beam the otter trawl had two thick iron shod boards, eight or ten feet long, one each side of the trawl mouth. As the strain came on the warp the otter boards swam outwards pulling the wings of the net with them. It was found that this contrivance could spread the net nearly twice as wide as the beam trawl, giving it an opening of 300 to 400 square feet in which to scoop up greater quantities of fish. The otter boards were also easier to handle than the beam and as they trailed above the bottom and not on it, they reduced the amount of damaged gear and lost fishing time caused by fouling obstructions.

It was reckoned that a steam trawler with the otter could catch eight and a half times as much as a sailing smack with a beam trawl.

Methods of drift net fishing did not change very much as a result of steam, but the speed with which a non-stop shuttle service between the fishing grounds and the quayside market could be maintained certainly did. Thus productivity increased because more time was spent actually fishing while the season lasted.

All round steam had brought immensely more catching power and the demand seemed as insatiable as the source of supply was prolific.

Since the discovery of the famous Silver Pits in 1843 the North Sea had been bottomless in its bounty. In the early years of this century 800,000 tons of white fish each year were being taken from it, over half of that by Britain. Anxieties about long term effects had been voiced at successive Royal Commissions and Parliamentary Committees over the years, but as expert opinion was always divided and as landings continued to go up in quantity, if down in quality, there was little stomach for restrictive legislation.

While the bumper harvest of 1913 was being landed nine nations met to set up a Council for a joint scientific investigation into the problem of overfishing. Soon after they had agreed a programme of research Germany withdrew her delegate and the whole question suddenly got a four year rest. Fortunately so did the fish.

● Alongside in the foreground is one of the oddest steam drifters in the East Anglian herring fleet, *LT1183 Scadaun*. Her owner was the 4th Earl of Dunraven, a well known Victorian sporting peer who twice challenged for the America's Cup. He often took a trip in his drifter and also used her as a tender to his racing yachts. She had a splendid cabin fitted out as an owner's state room. *Scadaun* was built in 1912, the same year as *LT1170 Gleaner of the Seas* with the wheatsheaf emblem on her funnel, seen just coming into a berth.

The Steam Fishermen go to War

AT 8.15 p.m. on August 4th 1914, the first day of the war, an Admiralty messenger walked across Whitehall to the Board of Agriculture and Fisheries with orders that no fishing vessel must be allowed to leave North Sea ports, and those at sea were to be ordered home by wireless. Hardly any fishing boats had wireless so this was easier said than done.

The instructions were relayed by telegraph to the Harbour Masters along the East Coast who were left to communicate as best they could. There were hundreds of steam drifters off the Yorkshire coast where the summer herring fishery was at its height. The trawler fleets were scattered across the thousands of square miles of sea which, for the past century, the Pax Brittanica had kept undisturbed "for such as pass on the seas upon their lawful occasions", as the Royal Navy's special prayer puts it. From Lowestoft alone there were on that day 220 sailing smacks strung between the Dowsing and the Gab and a steam trawler was sent to try and round them up.

Seven eighths of the country's fish supply was landed at the ports bordering the North Sea, sometimes known as the German Ocean, which was about to become the point of impact for two massive iron clad navies. The Admiralty wanted the pitch cleared.

Within a day or two the harbours were congested with boats and bewildered men wondering what would happen next. At Lowestoft and Yarmouth thousands of barrels of salted herring clogged the quayside as the weekly freighters from Hamburg failed to appear to take them away to the German importers who were the biggest customers. Two unfortunate and uninformed German fishing vessels sailed into Aberdeen to land fish and were promptly interned.

In previous wars the fishing communities had always been a prime source of naval cannon fodder, usually forcibly recruited by the press gangs, but the 20th century Navy had to think of more civilised methods. In 1911 it had formed a special Trawler Section of the Royal Naval Reserve and had invited skippers to undertake naval training. At the same time 100 first class steam trawlers were earmarked for instant requisition in the event of an outbreak of war.

The need for trawlers arose mainly from a devilish new development in naval warfare, the sea mine, first tried in the Crimean War but now much more sophisticated. Trawlers might have been purpose built as an antidote to this new weapon, for the skills and the gear needed for towing minesweeping paravanes is not much different to that for towing trawls.

As the fleets steamed back to port to await events Captain A.A. Ellison, R.N. set up his desk in the pavilion on Lowestoft South Pier to take command of the minesweeping squadron. He was none too soon. The enemy had already, on the first day of the war, sowed the first mines off Southwold.

● New meets old. The smack is *LT382 Gertrude* close hauled and double reefed in a smart blow. The steam trawler from which the photograph was taken is unidentified but the retired Lowestoft shipwright, Mr. Ted Frost thinks she is Dutch built from the shape of the focsle companionway top.

The original 100 earmarked craft soon proved inadequate to the task — an extremely hazardous one because there was no operational experience in tackling this menace. In a lightning operation of just 11 days a further 100 steam trawlers were requisitioned and fitted out to clear and buoy safe channels along the coastal shipping routes.

Even then nobody envisaged the extent of the part which would be played in the naval war of 1914-18 by the steam fishing fleets. Before the end of the conflict the industry had provided the Royal Navy with over 3,000 vessels (after a bit of haggling over charter rates) 49,000 men (about half the total of fishermen) and countless acts of heroism (including two V.C's).

At first the skippers recruited to the naval reserve were a bit of an embarrassment to Their Lordships. Here were men excelled in seamanship, used to danger and in the habit of undisputed command, yet who spoke not with the accents of Osborne and Dartmouth. They couldn't be ratings, but could they be officers? The problem was solved by creating the commissioned rank of Chief Skipper.

Walter Wood who in 1919 wrote a book called 'Fishermen In Wartime' said that the war had changed many people out of recognition, but no change was more outstanding than that of "the grim skipper who had sported a battered bowler, an intensely fishy dopper and enormous clompers, who gravitated when travelling to the third class smoker, turned gold braided, blue clad Chief Skipper with a place on the Navy List and a first class pass when travelling by train".

Further down the ladder the ex-fishermen deck hands of minesweepers and patrol vessels were regarded at first with an equal suspicion by regular ratings and petty officers, for their intense independence gave them a devil may care attitude to the niceties of uniform and other manifestations of service discipline. However, it did not take long to see that they were the first to dash into danger with the same careless disregard. "Don't worry about us, we're used to being drowned" was a wry fisherman's saying they often quoted.

The Admiralty had originally intended to requisition only trawlers for naval service, but presently they found an unexpected use for drifters and took them over in hundreds too. The secret was that they had men skilled in laying a line of submerged nets up to two miles long and fishing with them in close proximity without becoming (except rarely) all snarled up together. The Navy found that if a fleet of drifters could shoot nets one after the other so that they were overlapping, mile after mile, they could gently and cunningly discover the perimeters of an enemy minefield. Using the same techniques they could also make a barrage capable of ensnaring submarines or the propellers of surface craft which tried to pass. A dozen drifters could block off the Dover Straits.

Such services were performed not just in home waters but, as the war progressed, in other theatres of operation too. It was in one of these that Skipper Joseph Watt earned one of the two V.C's won by fishermen in the 1914 war.

Skipper Watt from Fraserburgh had taken the local built *Gowan Lea,* 35 tons and 27 horse power, to the Adriatic where a drifter line was employed in the Straits of Otranto. On the morning of May 15th 1917 these little ships were attacked by Austrian light cruisers, one of which came to within 100 yards range of the *Gowan Lea* and ordered the crew to abandon ship.

Skipper Watt called on his men to cheer and fight to the finish with their solitary six pounder gun, at the same time ringing on the telegraph for full steam ahead and dodging as best he could. A shot from the cruiser crippled the six pounder, but the gun crew, some of them wounded, continued to try and get it working while under a hail of fire. With his gun out of action, crew wounded and ship damaged Skipper Watt did not drop out of the fight, but steamed to the assistance of other drifters which were now under the cruiser's fire, some of which were sinking. Fourteen of them went down in the

● Solid ranks of funnels in the Waveney Dock in the 1930's. In the foreground is the steel drifter-trawler *LT188 Tritonia* which was later fitted with a diesel engine. In 1960 when fishing in the Bristol Channel under Skipper Toddy Green she brought up in her trawl the cavel of the Lowestoft sailing smack *Trevose* sunk in that spot by a German U-boat 44 years earlier. A cavel was a rail to hold belaying pins across the transom of a smack and carried the vessel's name. Beyond *Tritonia* is *LT246 Neves,* then *Playmates,* originally a Yarmouth boat built at Selby in 1925, later owned by J. J. Colby of Pakefield. She went missing with all hands in March 1955 when mackerel fishing off the Cornish coast with a relief skipper Jimmy Jenner. Beyond her is another J.J. Colby owned drifter *Sunbeam II* locally built in 1916.

Straits of Otranto that day with a loss of 67 hands. Five other skippers in the action received the Distinguished Service Cross.

The other fishing V.C. of the war was won in a sailing smack by the legendary Lowestoft skipper Tom Crisp of the *Nelson*. He already had the D.S.C. for sinking two submarines and died in a gallant engagement with another. This is the only case in the annals of the Victoria Cross where father and son were together in the action for which the award was made, for the mate of the *Nelson* was his 17 year old son Tom Crisp, Junior, who took over command from his dying father and brought the crew to safety in the smack's small boat. He was afterwards commissioned himself and received his father's V.C. from King George V, as well as the D.S.M. for himself. After a long and active life he slipped quietly to his final anchorage as this book was being written.

The David and Goliath escapades of the sailing smacks in the First World War are rather more frequently recalled than the exploits of the steam fishermen, partly because the former acted independently while more of the latter were organised in naval units. Gallant though the little brown sailed smacks were however, it was numerically a steam fisherman's war and the records contain scores of tales of their heroism. Neither were such deeds confined to vessels serving with the Navy. Those who continued fishing frequently found themselves in the front line.

672 trawlers and drifters were sunk and 416 lives lost through enemy action while engaged in fishing, quite apart from the hundreds whose names went to swell the Royal Navy casualty lists. Despite this the 14,000 men still left fishing (the balance had gone into the army or jobs ashore) succeeded in contributing 400,000 tons to the nation's food supply every year of the war.

It was, of course, essential that fishing should go on to help feed the population, but it was not made easy. The Admiralty were reluctant to let to sea ships they could not adequately protect, especially such sitting targets as fishing boats encumbered by their nets. Permits to fish were needed and by the end of the war there was a maze of 70 different sorts of permit. Being competitive hunters by nature the fishermen did not take easily to the various schemes that were made for working in limited areas or fishing in convoy under gunboat protection. The constant cry of the fishermen was for guns so they could look after themselves. When they eventually got them they used them to very good effect.

There was a case of the lone Yarmouth drifter *L.F.S.* which was attacked by five German sea planes and brought down two of them. The Humber steam trawlers *Conan Doyle* and *Sylvania* were engaged in classic actions protecting unarmed sister ships while fishing in convoy off the Shetlands. Between 20 and 30 U-boats were believed to have been sunk by armed trawlers in the four years of war.

Some steam trawlermen could become quite stroppy if not given a chance of mixing fishing with fighting as this disarming letter to the Admiralty from a firm of Welsh owners shows:—

"We would like to call your attention to the fact that your authorities at Cardiff have at least twice stopped our armed trawlers from going to sea because submarines were in the Channel. This is the very time we ought to be allowed out, for our two trawlers, armed as they now are, should beat any single submarine and make a good fight with two at once. Our men were indignant at being stopped from going to sea. Our men are very keen from patriotism and revenge and they also like the awards we give them for fighting submarines".

At the height of the herring season there was fierce competition to land the catch while prices were high and be off to sea again. There was no system. The drifter that could get to the quay and make fast was the one that could unload. Docking was consequently accomplished with a good deal of noisy exchange, which occasionally came to blows. At Yarmouth ships lay alongside the long length of quays in the river, but congestion was worse in Lowstoft's dock where it was often only possible to moor bow-to, a position which made unloading more arduous. As everybody had steam up ready to grab a chance of a berth the harbour was often hidden in a pall of smoke in the heyday of steam. With her bow against the lamppost is *LT106 Try Again*, in her day the fastest drifter in the port. In the next berth is *LT1065 Breadwinner* built in 1907 and owned by J.H. Jenner of Kessingland. Pushing her way in between them is *YH562 Twelve*, a steel drifter built at North Shields in 1901. She belonged to the Smiths Dock Trust Limited which before the First World War owned the biggest fleet in Yarmouth. They were all unromantically named with the number of their acquisition from *One* to *Thirty Three*. Beyond her is *LT609 Togo*, 28 tons, built at Fellow's yard in Yarmouth in 1905. During the 20's she fished out of Yarmouth as *YH248*, but in 1935 was converted to a diesel trawler and worked as a Lowestoft boat again until 1967.

Not all the fishing boats which took on submarines were armed. On the evening of August 16th 1915 the freighter *Matje* bound from Llanelly to Western Scotland with coal was attacked by a submarine. After a barrage of six or eight shots the crew were taking to the boats believing all to be lost. Suddenly they saw the steam trawler *Majestic*, belching smoke and making full speed to ram the sub which crash dived and made off. The *Majestic* carried no gun and there was no naval patrol help to call on within half an hour's steaming.

Rescuing survivors from merchantmen hit by mines or torpedoes was another job which wartime steam fishing fleets took in their stride. A typical example was when men of the Lowestoft drifters *Hilda & Ernest* (Skipper Ernest Snowline) and *Eager* (Skipper William Allerton) searched in a minefield for survivors from the *S.S. Gulliver*, putting themselves in great personal peril.

The fishermen were in no doubt about the risks they took, for there grew up a particular emnity between the U-boats and the fishermen. In the eyes of the U-boat captains fishing vessels when armed forfeited considerations generally accorded to crews of civilian vessels.

There was the case of the Grimsby trawler *Nemo* attacked while searching for survivors from her sister ship *Vanilla* which had been torpedoed without warning. There were stories of fishermen being taken from their small boats, which were then sunk, and lined up on the casing of the U-boats and left there to drown as they submerged.

Whether carrying on fishing or serving in naval units the steam fishermen played a vital role in what the next generation always knew as The Great War. The price of fish, as of practically everything else, soared during the war, but it is doubtful if the British public ever realised its true cost any more than it did in peace time.

Rudyard Kipling tried to do the wartime fishermen justice in a poem called "The Lowestoft Boat"

"They gave her government coal to burn
And a QF gun at her bow and stern.
And sent her out a roving
The Lord knows where"

went one verse. Unfortunately it was not one of the more inspired efforts of the master of patriotic verse.

Admiral Lord Jellicoe made a less poetic but more practical appraisal. He said: "The Grand Fleet could not have existed without the trawlers".

● Landing mackerel at Lowestoft. Mackerel fishing was more of a gamble than herring fishing, but very profitable if successful. The fleet of nets used was higher in the water and twice as long as for herring, sometimes up to 2½ miles. Hundreds of East Coast drifters went west in the spring for the Cornish mackerel season.

LANDING MACKEREL. LOWESTOFT.

The Last Years of Steam

EVEN BEFORE they sailed to war the steam fishing fleets had a rival. Mr. Gardner had perfected his diesel engine in Manchester in 1894 and just after the turn of the century experiments were made in fitting these to fishing craft. At first they could not develop enough power for the job, but this soon changed and by 1908 marine internal combustion engines had a distinct foot in the door.

Among the diesel pioneers were *FR158 Vineyard* and the Eyemouth boat *BK146 Maggie Jane's*. This innovation was one in which Scotland, and in particular Eyemouth, led the way. They were quick to see the advantage of engines which did not have to be constantly fed by a strong pair of arms, of a fuel that was easier to handle and neater to stow and which didn't leave dust everywhere. Above all they discovered it cut their running costs in half. For a start there were no stoker's wages.

Even back in 1881 at the launching of the first Grimsby steam trawler one of the company's directors prophesied in his speech that the new wonder would soon be superceded by a greater. He said that the time was not far distant when their vessels "would go out filled with electricity and return with the treasures of the deep". If he was a little hazy on technical detail the general sentiment was not far out.

Scotland had a hundred motor vessels by 1913 and the Continental countries concentrated on the same development rather than the expansion of their steam fleets. The English ports remained for a long time faithful to steam. It was 1926 before Richards yard at Lowestoft laid down its first motor drifter, the *Veracity*. The previous year the yard had launched what were to be its last pair of steam fishing vessels, the drifters *Forecast* and *Charter,* and that was only a year after building their last sailing smack *Arum Lily.*

The war encouraged rather than held back the growth of motor power. As so many steam vessels were serving with the Navy, the Board of Agriculture and Fisheries provided subsidies to help hundreds of the smaller inshore fishing craft then under sail to install auxiliary motors in order to keep fish supplies going.

When the steam fishermen were demobilised and returned to their home ports many of them were no doubt thinking of the last glorious herring season of 1913, but they were in for a bitter disappointment. Despite the respite from Man's predations the post war herring harvests never reached expectations and continued to be patchy through the 20's. The very last year remembered as a reasonable season for herring was 1929, since when the industry has been in steady decline and today has virtually vanished altogether and with it a whole way of life for the coastal communities.

The lack of herring was not the only difficulty which faced the fishermen after 1918. The market went sick too and they could not always sell what they had caught. The German export trade which had been so major a portion of the pre-war sales did not resume with anything like its former volume and Russia, the next biggest customer, was unsettled in the aftermath of the Revolution. To make matters worse the home market also showed a dramatic decline. The British palate began to disdain the cheap but highly nutritious herring and the reason was the growth of that great British contribution to civilisation, the fish and chip shop.

● The men who went to sea in the steam fishing fleets were only a fraction of those who earned their living from it. The jobs of thousands of shipwrights, netmakers, coopers, carters, curers and many more tradesmen also depended on the fishing. An important link in the chain were the beatsters seen above, who repaired herring nets when they were beyond the minor running repairs carried out at sea. As a drifter shot a line or 'fleet' of nets a mile or more long their make-up and upkeep was a complex business. The nets consisted of long narrow sections called 'lints' joined together horizontally, four or five at a time, to make up a net some 100 yards long by 14 yards deep. Over a score of these were joined together to make a 'fleet'. After the beatsters had done their work the nets were overhauled and made ready for sea by a 'ransacker'. In the early sailing days nets were made of hemp, but during the steam era were made from machine knitted cotton. Each few trips they were barked or tanned to prevent rot.

● The huge concentrations of drifters in the herring season meant that on any night there would be thousands of miles of net down in the North Sea in close proximity. Occasionally a sudden shift in the weather would lead to a snarl-up. In a bad case nets would have to be cut away and lost. Minor tangles were sorted out on the homeward voyage, but sometimes what the fishermen called a frap would have to be dealt with ashore. The cost of a fleet of herring nets between the wars was £400 to £500. Loss and damage hit the Scotsmen more than their English counterparts because they worked to a system where the crew owned the nets. Because of this it sometimes happened that a gale would leave several hundred families with severe financial problems.

By 1920 there were among the terraced houses of the industrial towns, 25,000 of these establishments where husband and wife proprietors busily battered and fried a grand total of 150,000 tons per annum of the poorer quality white fish, about one fifth of the total trawler landings. In Sheffield alone it was estimated that the fish and chip shops were providing steelworkers and their families with 400,000 square meals a week, at an average cost of a shilling (5p) a meal.

Their role in providing mass cheap nutrition in the depression years which followed was a minor economic miracle, but that did not help the herring men whose depression was as great as anyone's. Those heady early years of steam with its greater efficiency had seen a pattern of less jobs and greater profits. Now there were fewer jobs still and a decline in profits as well. Hundreds of steam drifters were broken up or left to rot and there was no money to replace worn out ships and gear. In 1913 1,500 steam drifters had earned £2,400 a piece. By 1933 there were but a thousand and they earned only an average of £1,100 each. The drifter owners of 1913 had prided themselves that with their modern steam vessels the all time record catch had been made by 25,000 men, just half the number there had been in 1880 when the fleets were one hundred per cent sail. By 1933 the number had fallen to 15,000.

On the Scots boats in that year men were said to be earning less than £1 a week, compared with £6 a week in 1913 when the pound was worth more. Even that was better than in a number of earlier years when they had settled in debt at the end of the season.

During these lean years there was a development that drove a further nail into the coffin of the herring fishery. A German skipper, Johanne von Eitzen of Hamburg, invented a trawl with a small third otter board centrally placed so that it pulled the mouth of the net upwards, enabling it to scoop up great quantities of paeligic fish, including herring which fed at certain times of day nearer the bottom. The trawled herring were inferior and often included a high percentage of immature fish and the driftermen were rightly concerned for their stocks. At Wick the skipper of the *Strathnaver* who brought the first trawled herring into the harbour was stoned by angry drifter crews, but for some years the practice went on.

The steam trawler skippers who took off their gold braid in 1918 came back to an altogether rosier future than their drifter brothers. The war had indeed proved the conservationists' point so far as demersal fish were concerned. North Sea grounds which had made the fortunes of 19th century smack owners, but which had been showing diminishing returns before the war, were once again teeming with cod, plaice and haddock. The steam trawlers were landing well over twice the catches they had before the war and this without the economic benefits of fleeting which was prohibited in wartime and not revived.

Every year the annual returns showed an increase in the total white fish landings, but statistics can breed a false sense of security. The fact was that nature's restorative work in the four-year rest period was wiped out again in another four by the catching power of the steam trawlers. Before long British trawlers were scraping the sea bed from the Moroccan Coast to Bear Island and the Barents Sea in search of new reserves. Government committees and international conferences discussed the question of overfishing but never devised effective action, just as today we talk about diminishing energy resources, but are never prepared for present restraint.

Ahead of its time in marketing techniques, the British Trawler Federation kept up demand with an "Eat More Fish" campaign launched in 1929. They produced wall charts and films for schools showing how fish was caught, and gave away fish recipe books, while they sent their skippers scouring ever more distant waters.

The demands of this far flung fishing were now more than the coal burning steam trawler could meet. In the 1920's they were usually about 175 feet long with triple expansion engines, a bunker capacity of 250 tons and holds to carry around 60 tons of fish. They had originally been built for six day voyages no more than 100 miles from home, but the majority of the voyages by the 30's were taking three or four weeks. Fewer ships with bigger tonnages made economic sense. Diesel engines became sufficiently powerful to drive big trawlers and the demise of steam began. It was a gradual replacement with none of the gold rush atmosphere which accompanied the change over from sail in the 1880's. Good steam engines take a long time to wear out. When the Second World War broke out in 1939 the Admiralty could still find some 300 coal burning drifters and trawlers to requisition.

The handful of sailing smacks remaining and working at that time ended their lives, usefully but sadly, as harbour barrages. Many of the steam fishing craft returned to work again after the war but by 1950 they were dwindling fast and the last of the era of steam survived the last of the sail by less than 30 years. Steam had come and gone in the compass of one fisherman's lifetime.

Unfortunately little remains as a reminder of this important era of our maritime heritage — even less than surviving examples of the sailing smacks and far less than the relics of the golden age of steam railways.

Only one steam drifter survives, *YH89 Lydia Eve* in the care of the National Maritime Trust. So far as one can discover no one has rescued a steam trawler for posterity.

Nevertheless there are many who remember and regret the passing of the steam fishing craft. Their engines had a grace of movement that produced power smoothly, quietly and almost effortlessly and they belonged to that less hurried and uncomplicated age when fathers on holiday were still able to maintain their esteem by explaining to their sons how such technical wonders worked, after no more than a brief crib at "Every Man His Own Mechanic".

The steam drifters and trawlers and the men who sailed them served the country magnificently in war and peace for 80 years and deserve their place in the national memory.

● Every year hundreds of Scottish boats sailed south for the autumn fishery. After the turn of the century the black sailed, lugger rigged fifies and zulus, nicknamed 'runties' by the East Anglian men, were quickly replaced by steam. Below *BF175 Dunedin* entering harbour on the right passes *BF167 Sunnyside*. Both were built in 1910. Above *BF336 Milky Way* also of 1910 vintage, built in Fraserburgh, and in the centre of the picture *BF922 Blossom*. None of the Scots fishermen fished or put to sea on Sunday. Most English skippers were not so strict, but those who were flew special 'Bethel' pennants at the masthead to show they had taken a pledge not to break the Sabbath.

● In the summer of 1930 Ford Jenkins took his camera on a trawling voyage out of Hull to Bear Island, a 1,500 mile journey taking 5½ days each way. The trip was in *H475 Lord Hewart,* 134 net tons, 96 h.p., built a couple of years earlier at Selby. She was one of several Lords of Hull owned by Pickering & Haldane's Steam Trawling Co. Limited, and is seen above in St. Andrew's Dock, Hull with *H32 Lord Lonsdale* and *H151 Lord Islington.* The whaleback focsle had just come in, affording at last a modicum of protection for men working on deck for long hours. The short sequence of photographs which follows are a record of the *Lord Hewart's* trip, but two pictures from a similar occasion have been included to give a complete idea of the trawling operation.

● *Lord Hewart* was trawling in 98 fathoms. Hauling in the steel wire trawl warp, anything up to 3,000 yards long, was done by the steam winch, but the final haul to heave the trawl aboard still involved muscle power. As the gear is brought aboard the cod end floats to the surface. The further from the ship it bobs up the better the bag is likely to be. A hand leans over to make fast the jiltson with which to hoist the cod end up above the deck.

● As the cod end swings inboard the mate unties the cod-end knot and releases the slithering pile of cod, catfish and halibut (the latter 'the pheasant of the sea' and fetching a high price). The large object hanging down is the cowhide which protected the bottom of the cod end as it was dragged along the sea bed. Before the men started to gut, ice and stow the catch the trawl would be shot again ready to be hauled a couple of hours later as soon as they had finished with the first catch. Work for the seven days spent on the grounds was therefore virtually non stop and men fell asleep where they stood, gutting knife in hand. At this latitude it was endless day in summer though the temperatures never rose over 40°F. In winter, in continual darkness, hot water had to be pumped all the time over winches and warps to stop them freezing solid.

● Back in the Humber the Custom's launch comes alongside, though the trawlermen's opportunities of acquiring illicit contraband must have been slender. The catch has been an exceptionally good one, 2,200 'kits' (the Humber ports measure), or 22,000 stones. *Lord Hewart's* skipper was a Pole called Russian Alec, one of the top men of the day and earning around £2,000 a year. The barrels on deck are some of the 55 casks of cods livers taken on the trip. These were crew's perks and sold for cod liver oil at 17s 6d a cask, to make an extra £4 for each man on top of his wages and 'poundage', or share of the profits.

● The *Lord Hewart's* stoker or trimmer comes up for a breath of well earned fresh air. In the course of the 18 day trip he had shovelled nearly 250 tons of coal, consumption being 12 tons a day. To enable such a weight to be carried some of it was bunkered for the outward voyage in the fishrooms, which had to be thoroughly cleaned out before trawling started. The average drifter used only about 15 tons of coal a week, as they needed their engines only to and from the grounds.

● *LT1299 Lavinia L,* a Catchpole owned boat launchèd in 1917, is starting her nets as she runs down wind, her mizzen sheet freed. She is shooting on the starboard side which was the custom. In explanation the drifter men would refer you to the story of the miraculous draft of fishes in St. John, Chapter 21, when Jesus told the disciples, "Cast the net on the right side of the ship and ye shall find". It was also traditional for skippers to give the order to shoot the nets with the words "Heave the nets in the name of the Lord" or just "Over for the Lord". The photograph above, though taken towards the end of the herring era, reflects the anxiety of skippers down the years. He is 'looking for appearances', the tell tale signs such as slight changes in the colour of the sea that indicated a swim of herring. On the left nets are being hauled. The East Anglian men would not talk about a catch but of a "shimmer" — it might be a good shimmer or a little shimmer. Occasionally it was known for there to be such a heavy shimmer as to endanger the vessel and some of the nets would have to be cut away.

● The tall thin funnels of the early steam fishing boats were dubbed
'Woodbine' funnels for their resemblance to the popular cigarette of
the day. This one is *LT161 Success* of 1900, only the eighth steamer
to be built by Samuel Richards. The photograph was probably taken
about 1902 soon after the launch of *LT60 Star of Hope* on the extreme
left, as only half a dozen funnels can be picked out among the thick
forest of masts in the dock beyond.

The bowler hat was common working gear in Edwardian times. Ashore it was the mark of the foreman and manager, but skippers sported them ashore and afloat. The long oilskin garment of the chap on the left is a dopper. After landing the bulk of the catch from *LT629 Request* the crew are cleaning the nets of the remains of the last haul. The *Request*, 38 tons and 15 h.p. was built in 1901 for the Star Drift Fishing Co.

● Only a quarter of the piles of herring landings seen here at Lowestoft market would be eaten fresh. The remainder went to curers who prepared it in various ways, mostly for export. The biggest customers were the merchants of Altona near Hamburg who bought the herring in boxes after it had been sprinkled with salt when fresh, a process known as klondyking. These fish were further processed on arrival in Germany for delicatessen. The Baltic countries were the next most important customers and the Russian ship *Ufa* above is loading the kind of herring preferred in that market — the 'Scotch cure', which meant barelling in brine after heading and gutting. Trawler landings were almost wholly for home consumption and with the help of ice stayed fresh for much longer than the paelegic fish. The railways were the key to distribution. All the rail companies had large special departments to handle fish traffic, mostly in special trains which shifted half a million tons a year. Thirteen fish trains a day used to leave Grimsby, each hauling 20 to 30 wagons, and took precedence over all other traffic on the Great Central. In the 1930's the public were paying 4½d (less than 2p) a pound for their herring, a shilling a pound (5p) for cod, while beef was two shillings a pound.

SCOTCH FISHER GIRLS GIPPING HERRINGS

● If the British public knew nothing else of the great days of steam drifters it knew of the famous Scots fisher girls who followed the herring's seasonal cycle, beginning as far north as Lerwick in the spring, progressing through Scotland and Northumberland in the early summer, on to Scarborough and Bridlington by August and culminating in East Anglia in the autumn. They worked in teams of three, two gutting and one packing. With their razor sharp knives flashing at lightning speed they could deal with as many as 50 herring a minute. The fish were first sprinkled with salt otherwise they would have been too slippery to handle at such speed. In the 1930's there were over 4,000 of the girls in East Anglia for the autumn season. The curers who employed them paid their travelling expenses and a substistance allowance. Then they received a weekly wage of about 17s 6d plus a shilling a barrel. On being engaged they also received a payment called 'arles', a sort of goodwill token of ten shillings or sometimes a pound. They would take home about an average of £20 each for their 8 to 10 weeks in Yarmouth or Lowestoft. They were always referred to as "fisher girls" regardless of age, but as the Jenkins collection of photographs shows a high proportion of them were goodlooking young women. It is not surprising that quite a number of today's Norfolk and Suffolk grandmothers first came south after the herring and stayed to marry.

50

FILLING HERRING BAR

● In addition to being Scotch cured and klondyked herring were also made into kippers, bloaters and red herrings. Kippers were the invention of a Newcastle man, John Woodger who settled in Yarmouth, about the middle of the 19th century. On the left herring intended for kippering are being placed on racks in the smoke house after being split and lightly salted. They were then smoked over fires of oak chippings and sawdust for about 10 days. The bloater, invented about the same time by a Yarmouth curer called Bishop, is left whole and is more lightly smoked. Red herrings (which were not red but a golden brown), were not popular in Britain but mainly exported to Mediterranean countries. These were soaked in brine and then smoked for a long time.

SQUIRREL

● As international competition in fishing became intense and trawling grounds more extended the need to protect British interests led to the formation of the Fishery Protection Service of the Royal Navy. *HMS Squirrel*, above, was an early member and there have been several of the name since. Of later vintage were *HMS Dee* and *HMS Cherwell*, above right. Another naval visitor to the fishing port, *HMS Halcyon* entertains regatta day crowds with a tiny replica of herself.

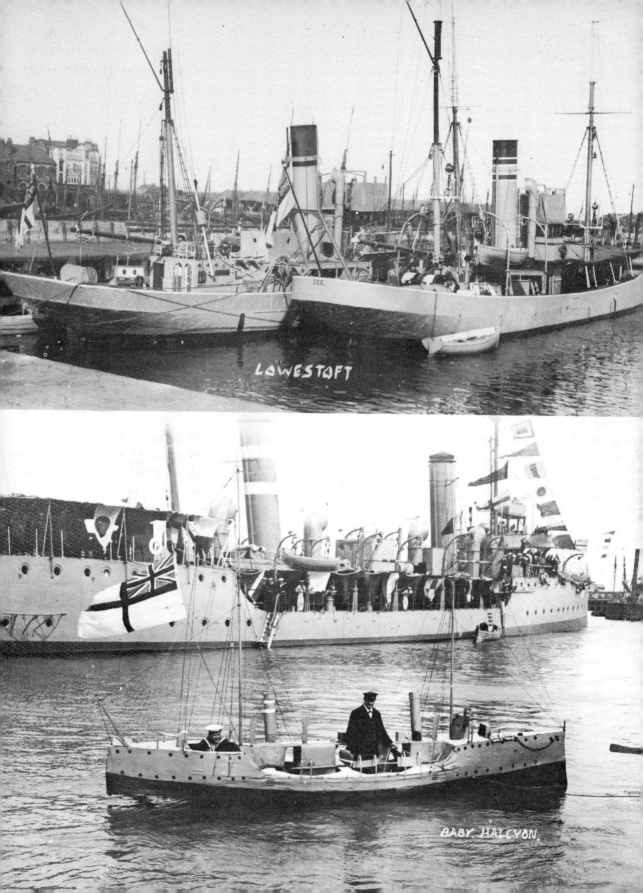

LOWESTOFT

BABY HALCYON.

● A German steam trawler, the *Hornskift* of Vesermunde working off Bear Island in 1930. The German steam trawler fleet developed rapidly in the first decade of the century and was mostly fishing Icelandic waters and landing catches at Aberdeen. By 1913 German trawlers accounted for a third of all trawled fish going into Aberdeen. By the time the fishing fleets converted to steam most of the merchant shipping companies had already done so, but sail remained stubbornly alive for many more years and steam fishermen on the grounds would often have a wave for a fine square rigger. This is *Celtic Glen* and the state of her topsides suggest she is nearing the end of a long voyage. She had a long life trading all over the globe under various names until she struck an iceberg and sank in 1926.

● Built as combined trawler and drifter *LT246 Neves* on her trial trip.
The year is 1913 and cloche hats are in evidence among the party
aboard. Her name spells backwards the name of the owners, Seven
Limited.

● The railways, which brought the coal for the steam fishing fleets and carried its bumper catches to inland markets, also brought seaside holidays within the reach of thousands and a new industry developed. This is Edwardian Southwold. Hotels like the Marlborough in front of the lighthouse were for the grand, but fishermen's wives were glad to earn a few extra shillings taking in visitors of the artisan class during the summer.

● By the time the combined drifter trawler *LT201 Quiet Waters* was launched in 1931 the aerial slung between the fore and mizzen masts had become common. By 1910 German owners had fitted half a dozen vessels with wireless, realising that this could convey not only gale warnings, but valuable market information, such as directing a homeward bound trawler to a port where auction prices were higher. British distant water trawlers did not have wireless until several years later. The wireless operators who shipped in them were employed by the Marconi Company, not the trawler owners. Transmissions cost 3½d to 7½d (1½ to 3 new pence) a word according to distance and were of course by key, not voice. Near water vessels had ordinary wireless receivers for sound broadcasts, the first to be fitted in Lowestoft being *Grey Sea* in the early 1920's. Above opposite, North Cone hoisted and the sea pounding against the most easterly coastguard station in England. A picture taken during the exceptional tidal surge of 1953 which caused extensive flooding on both sides of the North Sea. Below, a steam drifter making for home while a well reefed smack battles it out on the skyline. Long after steam had replaced sail the lifeboats which went to the aid of fishermen in distress remained lugger rigged sailing vessels. It was not until 1921 that the first motor lifeboat, *Agnes Cross*, went into service on the Lowestoft Station. There never was a steam lifeboat because it would have taken too long to get up a head of steam in emergency.

● Washing up the galley pans, the lot of ships boys the world over. As the age of steam progressed their life became better. The apprenticeship system, which often meant exploitation, was abandoned and regulations after 1920 prevented any boy under 16 being taken to sea, except in small inshore craft. In the early gold rush days of steam at Grimsby, when there was a shortage of hands, boys of 12 were shipped in scores, having been "apprenticed" from local orphanages. They were paid what the owners thought fit, which was hardly anything, and were grossly ill-treated. They could be goaled for deserting, but that did not stop 14% of them running from their ships as they found prison preferable. In ports where fishing was a family affair it was a different matter. Lads were usually eager to get to sea with their dads.

● For many years the famous London fish restaurant Madame Pruniers' awarded an annual trophy for the biggest single catch of herring. It was won in 1952 by Skipper Joe Thompson of *LT20 Lord Hood* seen above crossing the bar loaded to the gunwhales with 314¾ crans, the biggest single catch of herring ever recorded. Perhaps the most notable of all Lowestoft herring skippers was Jumbo Fiske, winner in 1964. The Prunier trophy is on the table while Skipper Fiske receives the masthead pennant to go with it from Lowestoft's Mayor, Councillor David Hayden.

● *LT1157 Sara Hide* and her sister ship *LT746 Margaret Hide* photographed together here were two of the best known steam fishing vessels of the later period at Lowestoft. They were built as dual purpose boats but were too under-powered to make successful trawlers. *Sara Hide* in her last days had a collision in the dock with *LT495 Lizzie West* which was the last steamer to fish from Lowestoft. She was bought from Buckie in 1930 and fished up to 1968. Powerful diesel trawlers like *LT371 Bryher* were the successors to the great age of steam. No old fisherman, either sail or steam, could complain of the grace of her lines, though the same cannot be said for the latest generation of stern trawlers.